Heart Song

Written By Melissa Guenthner
Illustrated By Lorraine Shulba

Heart Song by Melissa Guenthner
All Copyrights Melissa Guenthner
Illustrations By Lorraine Shulba
Published By Blue Bug Studios

ISBN: 978-1-9991679-3-6

To Luke born 1360 grams
For filling my heart with songs and my mind with dreams to chase.
You are my life's blessing and I wish this song for you.

Little Luke was born very small
Only half the size of other babies
But he was very, very tough
And his Mommy loved him with all her heart

Every night Mommy held him on her chest

Ba-bump...
Ba-bump...
Ba-bump...

And as they snuggled tight he heard

Ba-bump...
Ba-bump...
Ba-bump...

Mommy's heart sang to him

Ba-bump...
Ba-bump...
Ba-bump...

Grow big, grow strong, grow healthy

Ba-bump...
Ba-bump...
Ba-bump...

As he drifted off to sleep each night
he heard his Mommy's heart sing to him

Ba-bump... Ba-bump...
Ba-bump...

Sleep well, rest long, grow strong

Ba-bump... Ba-bump...
Ba-bump...

As he lay sleeping peaceful and warm

Mommy's heart song sang to him

Ba-bump...
        Ba-bump...
    Ba-bump...

Grow big, grow strong, grow healthy

Ba-bump...
        Ba-bump...
    Ba-bump...

And Luke did grow big, strong and healthy.

Listening to his Mommy's heart song

Ba-bump...
Ba-bump...
Ba-bump...

When he grew big enough to sleep in his own bed

He would close his eyes and hear

Ba-bump...
Ba-bump...
Ba-bump...

Sleep deep, dream big, grow strong-

Ba-bump...
Ba-bump...
Ba-bump...

Mommy's heart song still sang to him

As he grew from a boy to a man

Mommy's heart still sang to him their song

Ba-bump...
Ba-bump...
Ba-bump...

Be kind, be real, be you

Ba-bump...
Ba-bump...
Ba-bump...

Anywhere he was in life,
he could close his eyes and hear
Mommy's heart song singing to him-

Ba-bump...
Ba-bump...
Ba-bump...

You're big, you're strong, you're loved
for always by your Mom

Ba-bump...
Ba-bump...

Melissa is a mother of two, a small business owner and a rancher along side her husband. She is a believer that if kids could hear the song a mother's heart dreams for them they can find strength during struggles.

Heart Song is her wish to her children and she shares it for those who might not otherwise find the words.

Lorraine Shulba was born and raised in Alberta and began painting since she could hold a paintbrush. She has studied fine art at both Grant MacEwan University & the University of Alberta. Lorraine's work is in numerous public & private collections throughout Canada, the United States & England. She has been published in publications such as Prime-Time magazine, Synchronicity, See Magazine, & Scholastics Canada. She currently resides in Edmonton and can be seen skulking around coffee shops, sketch book in hand, waiting for inspiration. Lorraine loves commissions as well! Just ask!
A professional award-winning graphic designer as well, she loves to help her clients get noticed!
Please visit her website www. lorraineshulba.com
Design www.bluebugstudios.com

Ba-bump... Ba-bump...
Ba-bump...